Words From the Wise

Fool me once, shame on you; fool me twice, shame on me.

Chinese Proverb

Words From The Wise

Centuries of Proverbs to Live By

Selected by Arthur Wortman

Illustrated With Woodcuts

by Fritz Kredel

 Hallmark Crown Editions

A proverb is a short sentence based
on long experience.

Miguel de Cervantes

On Love
and
Friendship...

The supreme happiness of life
is the conviction that we are loved.
Victor Hugo

Words are the voice of the heart.
Confucius

Love looks not with the eyes, but
with the heart.
William Shakespeare

A smile is a light in the window
of a face that signifies the heart
is at home and waiting.
Anonymous

They who love are but one step
from Heaven.

James Russell Lowell

If love be timid it is not true.

Spanish Proverb

The conquest of passion gives
ten times more happiness
than we can reap from the
gratification of it.

Sir Richard Steele

Whatever is in the heart will
come up to the tongue.

Persian Proverb

He saith little that loveth much.

Italian Proverb

To find out a girl's faults, praise
her to her girl friends.

Benjamin Franklin

No wife can endure a gambling
husband, unless he is a
steady winner.

T.R. Dewar

The best way to know God is to
love many things.
Vincent van Gogh

All things whatsoever ye would
that men should do unto you, do
ye even so unto them.
New Testament

No human creature can give
orders to love.
George Sand

Though honey is sweet, do not
lick it off a briar.
Irish Proverb

God did not create woman from
man's head, that he should
command her, nor from his feet,
that she should be his slave, but
rather from his side, that she
should be near his heart.
Hebrew Proverb

Love is of all passions the
strongest, for it attacks
simultaneously the head, the
heart, and the senses.
Voltaire

Kindness in words creates
confidence; kindness in thinking
creates profoundness; kindness
in giving creates love.
Lao-Tse

Grief can take care of itself,
but to get the full value of a joy
you must have somebody to
divide it with.
Mark Twain

We make more enemies by
what we say than friends by
what we do.
John Collins

There is the same difference in a
person before and after he is in
love as there is in an unlighted
lamp and one that is burning.
Vincent van Gogh

One pardons to the degree that
one loves.

La Rochefoucauld

Every man can tell how many
goats or sheep he possesses, but
not how many friends.

Cicero

When a woman is speaking
to you, listen to what she says
with her eyes.

Victor Hugo

Think not those faithful who
praise all thy words and actions,
but those who kindly reprove
thy faults.

Socrates

Love is the reward of love.
Johann von Schiller

The riches that are in the heart
cannot be stolen.
Russian Proverb

Friendship will not continue to
the end which is begun for an end.
Francis Quarles

A mile walked with a friend has
only one hundred steps.
Russian Proverb

Who is the bravest hero? He who
turns his enemy into a friend.
Hebrew Proverb

10

Do not remove a fly from your
friend's head with a hatchet.
Chinese Proverb

Keep company with good men,
and you'll increase their number.
Italian Proverb

A good husband makes a good wife.
Robert Burton

Love is the business of the idle,
but the idleness of the busy.
Baron Lytton

A devoted friendship is never
without anxiety.
Marquise de Sévigné

11

If you go to war pray once; if you
go on a sea journey pray twice;
but pray three times when you
are going to be married.

Russian Proverb

Judge not thy neighbor until
thou art come into his place.

Hebrew Proverb

Hay smells different to lovers
and horses.

Anonymous

Every man should have a fair-
sized cemetery in which to bury
the faults of his friends.

Henry Ward Beecher

Better be alone than in bad company.

Anonymous

Few men are admired by their servants.

Michel Eyquem de Montaigne

One of the best ways to keep
friendship is to return it.

Anonymous

On Character...

It takes little effort to watch
a man carry a load.
Chinese Proverb

There's only one corner of the
universe you can be certain of
improving, and that's your
own self.
Aldous Huxley

When you can do the common
things of life in an uncommon
way, you will command the
attention of the world.
George Washington Carver

The gem cannot be polished
without friction, nor man
perfected without trials.
Chinese Proverb

If you tell the truth, you don't
have to remember anything.
Mark Twain

To live is to change, and to be
perfect is to have changed often.
Cardinal Newman

What sunshine is to flowers,
smiles are to humanity.
Joseph Addison

It is not only what we do, but
also what we do not do, for
which we are accountable.
Jean Molière

He who prizes little things is
worthy of great ones.
German Proverb

Winter comes fast on the lazy.
Irish Proverb

The great man is he who does not
lose his child's heart.
Anonymous

The measure of a man's real
character is what he would do
if he knew he would never be
found out.
Thomas Macaulay

Good example is half a sermon.
Anonymous

Children have more need
of models than of critics.
Joseph Joubert

You cannot do a kindness too
soon, because you never know
how soon it will be too late.
Anonymous

No man, for any considerable
period, can wear one face to
himself, and another to the
multitude, without finally getting
bewildered as to which may be the true.
Nathaniel Hawthorne

If you wish your merit to be known, acknowledge that of other people.

Oriental Proverb

He who closes his ears to the views of others shows little confidence in the integrity of his own views.

William Congreve

Is it progress if a cannibal uses knife and fork?

Anonymous

The girl who can't dance says the band can't play.

Yiddish Proverb

A book whose sale's forbidden all men rush to see, and prohibition turns one reader into three.

Italian Proverb

A cynic is a man who knows the price of everything and the value of nothing.

Oscar Wilde

When the fox cannot reach
the grapes he says they
are not ripe.

Greek Proverb

There is no comparison between
that which is lost by not
succeeding, and that which is
lost by not trying.

Francis Bacon

The best place to find a helping
hand is at the end of your
own arm.

Swedish Proverb

The greater the obstacle the more
glory in overcoming it.
Jean Molière

Rotten wood cannot be carved.
Chinese Proverb

He who falls in love with himself
will have no rivals.
Benjamin Franklin

They who give have all things;
they who withhold have nothing.
Hindu Proverb

He that leaveth nothing to chance
will do few things ill, but he will
do very few things.
Marquis of Halifax

You have not converted a man
because you have silenced him.
John, Viscount Morley

A man's faults all conform to his
type of mind. Observe his faults
and you may know his virtues.
Confucius

Terrifying are the weaknesses
of power.
Greek Proverb

The greatest prayer is patience.
Buddha

Goodness is the only investment
that never fails.
Henry David Thoreau

Borrow trouble for yourself, if
that's your nature, but don't lend
it to your neighbors.

Rudyard Kipling

He who limps is still walking.

Swiss Proverb

He who has no poetry in himself
will find poetry in nothing.

Joseph Joubert

The greatest thing in the world
is to know how to be yourself.

Michel Eyquem de Montaigne

One cannot tell what passes
through the heart of a man by
the look on his face.

Japanese Proverb

It is with narrow-souled people as with narrow-necked bottles: the less they have in them, the more noise they make in pouring it out.

Jonathan Swift

People who aren't afraid to roll up their sleeves seldom lose their shirts.

Anonymous

Tell a woman she is beautiful, and the devil will repeat it to her ten times.

Italian Proverb

This above all: to thine own self
be true, And it must follow, as the
night the day, Thou canst
not then be false to any man.
William Shakespeare

The more help a man has in his
garden, the less it belongs to him.
W.H. Davies

To attribute to a good man
merits which he does not have
is to fail to recognize those he has.
Joseph Joubert

Never ascribe to an opponent
motives meaner than your own.
James Barrie

Patience is the key to joy;
but haste is the key to sorrow.
Arabian Proverb

A reconciliation without an
explanation that error lay on
both sides is not a true
reconciliation.
Hebrew Proverb

A politician thinks of the next
election; a statesman, of the
next generation.
Paul Claudel

One man with courage makes
a majority.
Andrew Jackson

Valor lies just halfway between
rashness and cowardice.
Miguel de Cervantes

He who boasts of his descent is
like the potato; the best part of
him is underground.
French Proverb

We have two ears and one mouth
that we may listen the more and
talk the less.
Greek Proverb

As a solid rock is not shaken by
a strong gale, so wise persons
remain unaffected by praise
or censure.
Buddha

Labor to keep alive within your
breast that little spark of celestial
fire called Conscience.

George Washington

Conceit is God's gift to little men.

Anonymous

He who peeps in at his neighbor's
window may chance to lose
his eyes.

Arabian Proverb

Tact is the unsaid part of what
you think; its opposite, the
unthought part which you say.

Henry van Dyke

Experience is not what happens to
a man; it is what a man does with
what happens to him.
Aldous Huxley

The greatest pleasure is to do
a good action by stealth and
to have it found out by accident.
Charles Lamb

A hero is no braver than an
ordinary man, but he is brave
five minutes longer.
Ralph Waldo Emerson

Never let the bottom of your
purse or your mind be seen.
Anonymous

People seldom improve when
they have no other model but
themselves to copy after.
Oliver Goldsmith

Nothing prevents us from being
natural so much as the desire
to appear so.
La Rochefoucauld

Shun idleness. It is a rust that attaches itself to the most brilliant of metals.

Voltaire

Proverbs bear age, and he who would do well may view himself in them as in a looking glass.

Italian Proverb

The face of the enemy frightens me only when I see how much it resembles mine.

Anonymous

Look for a thing till you find it and you'll not lose your labor.

Chinese Proverb

A man shows his character by
what he laughs at.
German Proverb

The great thing in the world is
not so much where we stand, as
in what direction we are moving.
Oliver Wendell Holmes

All the beautiful sentiments in
the world weigh less than a
single lovely action.
James Russell Lowell

A man is rich in proportion to
the number of things which he
can afford to let alone.
Henry David Thoreau

Fear is the tax which conscience
pays to guilt.

Anonymous

A man who has committed a
mistake and doesn't correct it
is committing another mistake.

Confucius

Pray to be stronger men! Do not
pray for tasks equal to your
powers. Pray for powers equal to
your tasks.

Phillips Brooks

Let us say what we feel, and feel
what we say; let speech
harmonize with life.

Seneca

Vanity keeps persons in favor
with themselves who are out of
favor with all others.

William Shakespeare

Always do right; this will gratify
some people and astonish the rest.

Mark Twain

On Life...

Soldiers win battles and generals get the credit.

Napoleon Bonaparte

Dost thou love life? Then do not squander time, for that is the stuff life is made of.

Benjamin Franklin

The rung of a ladder was never meant to rest upon, but only to hold a man's foot long enough to enable him to put the other somewhat higher.

Thomas Huxley

A different world cannot be built
by indifferent people.
Anonymous

In the kingdom of the blind men,
the one-eyed man is king.
Anonymous

The one serious conviction that a
man should have is that nothing
is to be taken too seriously.
Samuel Butler

You will never get ahead trying
to get even.
Anonymous

A barking dog is often more
useful than a sleeping lion.
Arabian Proverb

Can anything be more ridiculous
than that a man should have the
right to kill me because he lives
on the other side of the water,
and because his ruler has
a quarrel with mine?
Blaise Pascal

Four things come not back—the
spoken word, the sped arrow, the
past life, and the neglected
opportunity.

Arabian Proverb

All work is as seed sown; it grows
and spreads and sows itself anew.

Anonymous

So live that you wouldn't be
ashamed to sell the family parrot
to the town gossip.

Will Rogers

Time and truth are friends,
though there are many moments
hostile to truth.

Joseph Joubert

You never know what is enough
until you know what is
more than enough.

William Blake

A guest has not to thank the host,
but the host the guest.

Russian Proverb

The vices are never so well
employed as in combating
one another.

William Hazlitt

When your horse is on the brink
of a precipice, it is too late to pull
the reins.

Chinese Proverb

As one may ascend to the
housetop by ladder, rope, or
bamboo, so there are many ways
to reach God.

Hindu Proverb

Make not a fence more expensive
or more important than the
thing that is fenced.

Hebrew Proverb

The liar's punishment is not in
the least that he is not
believed, but that he cannot
believe anyone else.

G. B. Shaw

To forget one's ancestors is to be a
brook without a source, a tree
without root.

Chinese Proverb

The cow knows not what her tail
is worth until she has lost it.

Anonymous

Justice without strength is helpless;
strength without justice
is tyrannical.

Blaise Pascal

Adversity is the diamond dust
Heaven polishes its jewels with.

Anonymous

Believe everything you hear
about the world; nothing is too
impossibly bad.

Honoré de Balzac

The world changes so fast that
one couldn't stay wrong all the
time if he tried.

Anonymous

There is no cure for birth or
death save to enjoy the interval.
George Santayana

Every generation laughs at the
old fashions, but follows
religiously the new.
Henry David Thoreau

A man who has work that suits
him and a wife he loves has
squared his accounts with life.
Friedrich Hegel

Justice is the insurance we have
on our lives, and obedience is the
premium we pay for it.
William Penn

It is useless for the sheep to pass
resolutions in favor of
vegetarianism while the wolf
remains of a different opinion.
W.R. Inge

A chameleon does not leave one
tree until he is sure of another.
Arabian Proverb

Some die too young, and some
die too old; the precept sounds
strange, but die at the right time.
Friedrich Nietzsche

If you have to kill a snake, kill
it once and for all.
Japanese Proverb

Better a sign which says
NO ENTRY than one which
says NO EXIT.
Anonymous

If God created shadows it was
in order to better emphasize
the light.

Pope John XXIII

All that is necessary for the
triumph of evil is for good men
to do nothing.

Edmund Burke

The journey of a thousand miles
starts with a single step.

Chinese Proverb

The grand essentials in this life are
something to do, something to
love, and something to hope for.

Joseph Addison

Men never do evil so completely
and cheerfully as when they do
it from religious conviction.

Blaise Pascal

Many who are ahead of their
time have to wait for it in
uncomfortable quarters.

Anonymous

Do not cut down the tree that
gives you shade.
Arabian Proverb

It is only when the cold season
comes that we know the pine
and cypress to be evergreens.
Chinese Proverb

The fall of a leaf is a whisper
to the living.
Russian Proverb

Nothing is more highly to be
prized than the value of each day.
Johann Wolfgang von Goethe

Talk does not cook rice.
Chinese Proverb

While we consider when to begin,
it becomes too late.
Latin Proverb

The path of duty lies in what is
near at hand; and men seek for it
in what is remote.
Japanese Proverb

Everything happens to everybody
sooner or later if there is
time enough.
G.B. Shaw

A man should learn to sail
in all winds.
Italian Proverb

Do you need to be told that
whatever has been, can still be?
Dag Hammarskjöld

He who plants thorns must never
expect to gather roses.
Arabian Proverb

Sorrow is a fruit: God does not
make it grow on limbs too weak
to bear it.
Victor Hugo

In a war of ideas it is people
who get killed.
Anonymous

He conquers who endures.
Italian Proverb

Let your hook be always cast;
in the pool where you least
expect it, there will be a fish.
>*Ovid*

The same fire purifies gold and
consumes straw.
>*Italian Proverb*

If you want anything done, give
it to the busy man.
>*Anonymous*

Some will shine in the second
rank who are lost in the first.
>*Voltaire*

He who rides a tiger is afraid
to dismount.
>*Chinese Proverb*

All things excellent are as
difficult as they are rare.
Benedict Spinoza

If the child does not cry, the
mother knows not its wants.
Russian Proverb

It is the beautiful bird
which gets caged.
Chinese Proverb

Success is a journey,
not a destination.
Anonymous

Be ashamed to die until you have
won some victory for mankind.
Horace Mann

The tragedy of life is not so
much what men suffer, but rather
what they miss.
Thomas Carlyle

Granting our wish is one of Fate's
saddest jokes.
James Russell Lowell

Fortune sometimes turns round
like a mill wheel and he who was
yesterday at the top lies today
at the bottom.
Miguel de Cervantes

The course of true anything
never does run smooth.
Samuel Butler

Forewarned, forearmed; to be
prepared is half the victory.
Miguel de Cervantes

Daring ideas are like chessmen
moved forward; they may be
beaten, but they may start a
winning game.
Johann Wolfgang von Goethe

The reward of a thing well done
is to have done it.
Ralph Waldo Emerson

When a man hasn't a good
reason for doing a thing, he has
a good reason for letting it alone.
Sir Walter Scott

43

Every cloud engenders not a storm.
William Shakespeare

If you walk on snow you cannot
hide your footprints.
Chinese Proverb

One father is more than a
hundred school masters.
George Herbert

There is a point at which even
justice does injury.
Sophocles

Bad neighbors count a man's
income, but not his expenses.
Hebrew Proverb

44

The pebble in the brook secretly
thinks itself a precious stone.
Japanese Proverb

Compare your griefs with other
men's and they will seem less.
Spanish Proverb

Everywhere in life the true
question is, not what we have
gained, but what we do.
Thomas Carlyle

I have always believed that good
is only beauty put into practice.
Jean Jacques Rousseau

You look for the horse you ride on.
Russian Proverb

It is no use to wait for your ship
to come in unless you have
sent one out.
Belgian Proverb

The dispensing of Injustice is
always in the right hands.
Anonymous

Think of the going-out before
you enter.
Arabian Proverb

The acts of this life are the
destiny of the next.
Oriental Proverb

He that wrestles with us
strengthens our nerves and
sharpens our skill.
Edmund Burke

What one does, one becomes.
Spanish Proverb

That is an empty purse that is
full of other men's money.
Anonymous

The great pleasure in life is doing
what people say you cannot do.
Walter Bagehot

One dog yelping at nothing will
set ten thousand straining at
their collars.
Japanese Proverb

Do not despise an insignificant enemy or a slight wound.
German Proverb

If young men had wit and old men strength everything might be well done.
Italian Proverb

For everything you have missed you have gained something else.
Ralph Waldo Emerson

The old begin to complain of the conduct of the young when they themselves are no longer able to set a bad example.
La Rochefoucauld

Castles in the air cost a vast deal to keep up.
Baron Lytton

The difference between the right word and the almost right word is the difference between lightning and the lightning bug.
Mark Twain

Eat vegetables and fear no creditors,
rather than eat duck and hide.
Hebrew Proverb

When the fruit is scarcest its
taste is sweetest.
Irish Proverb

What the young one begs for,
the grown-up throws away.
Russian Proverb

Thatch your roof before rainy
weather; dig your well before you
become parched with thirst.
Chinese Proverb

What is bitter to endure may be
sweet to remember.
Anonymous

Each goodly thing is hardest
to begin.
Edmund Spenser

To enjoy life, we must touch
much of it lightly.
Voltaire

On Happiness and Contentment...

Happiness is a butterfly, which when pursued, is always just beyond your grasp, but which, if you will sit down quietly, may alight upon you.

Nathaniel Hawthorne

There is no one luckier than he who thinks himself so.

German Proverb

Those who bring sunshine to the lives of others cannot keep it from themselves.

Sir James Barrie

He is happiest, be he king or
peasant, who finds peace in
his home.

Johann Wolfgang von Goethe

Happiness *is* virtue, not its reward.

Benedict Spinoza

Wrinkles should merely indicate
where smiles have been.

Mark Twain

He who allows his day to pass by
without practicing generosity
and enjoying life's pleasures is
like a blacksmith's bellows—he
breathes but does not live.

Sanskrit Proverb

God gave us our memories so
that we might have roses in
December.
Sir James Barrie

A long life may not be good
enough, but a good life is
long enough.
Anonymous

Let thy discontents be secrets.
Benjamin Franklin

Happiness is like a sunbeam,
which the least shadow intercepts,
while adversity is often as the
rain of spring.
Chinese Proverb

He who sings frightens away
his ills.
Spanish Proverb

He who reigns within himself,
and rules passions, desires, and
fears, is more than a king.
John Milton

Stand still, and consider the
wondrous works of God.
Old Testament

Good humor is one of the best
articles of dress one can wear
in society.
William Makepeace Thackeray

All of the animals except man
know that the principal business
of life is to enjoy it.
Samuel Butler

Be at war with your vices,
at peace with your neighbors,
and let every new year
find you a better man.
Benjamin Franklin

52

We overlook so much happiness,
because it costs nothing.
Anonymous

Anger is never without a reason,
but seldom with a good one.
Benjamin Franklin

Burdens become light when
cheerfully borne.
Ovid

Happy the generation where
the great listen to the small,
for it follows that in such
a generation the small will listen
to the great.

Hebrew Proverb

As long as the sun shines one
does not ask for the moon.

Russian Proverb

Unhappiness is not knowing
what we want and killing
ourselves to get it.

Anonymous

To be an agreeable guest one
need only enjoy one-self.

Joseph Joubert

When you jump for joy, beware
that no one moves the ground
from beneath your feet.

Anonymous

It's nice to be important, but
it's more important to be nice.

Anonymous

That day is lost on which one has
not laughed.
French Proverb

You cannot prevent the birds of
sadness from passing over your
head, but you can prevent their
making nests in your hair.
Chinese Proverb

He who fears death enjoys not life.
Spanish Proverb

The soul's greatest perfection is
its capacity for pleasure.
Anonymous

When we are happy we are
always good, but when we are
good we are not always happy.
Oscar Wilde

Fear less, hope more; eat less,
chew more; whine less, breathe
more; talk less, say more; hate
less, love more; and all good
things are yours.
Swedish Proverb

Everything in the world may
be endured except continual
prosperity.

Johann Wolfgang von Goethe

The art of living lies less in
eliminating our troubles than
in growing with them.

Bernard Baruch

Pleasure is often spoiled by
describing it.

Henri Stendhal

Joy and sorrow are next
door neighbors.

German Proverb

If there is righteousness in the
heart, there will be beauty in the
character. If there is beauty in
the character, there will be
harmony in the home. If there is
harmony in the home, there will
be order in the nation. If there is
order in the nation, there will be
peace in the world.

Chinese Proverb

On Wit
and
Wisdom...

An eel held by the tail is not
yet caught.

Anonymous

Who is wise? He who can learn
from every man.

Hebrew Proverb

The man who talks of an
unalterable law is probably
an unalterable fool.

Sydney Smith

Silence betokens consent.

Persian Proverb

Common sense in an uncommon
degree is what the world
calls wisdom.

> *Samuel Taylor Coleridge*

Those who know when they
have enough are rich.

> *Chinese Proverb*

No one is exempt from talking
nonsense; the mistake is to do
it solemnly.

> *Michel Eyquem de Montaigne*

Wise men talk because they have
something to say; fools, because
they have to say something.

> *Plato*

Don't marry for money; you can
borrow it cheaper.
Scottish Proverb

There is no opinion so absurd
but that some philosopher will
express it.
Cicero

Genius is one per cent inspiration
and ninety-nine per cent
perspiration.
Thomas Edison

It is useless for us to attempt to
reason a man out of a thing he
has never been reasoned into.
Jonathan Swift

Facts do not cease to exist because
they are ignored.

Anonymous

It's no use going to the goat's
house to look for wool.

Irish Proverb

He is a hard man who is only
just, and a sad one who is
only wise.

Voltaire

It is better to debate a question
without settling it than to settle
a question without debating it.

Joseph Joubert

The training which makes men
happiest in themselves also makes
them most serviceable to others.
John Ruskin

Very simple ideas lie within the
reach only of complex minds.
Remy de Gourmont

In the fields of observation,
chance favors only the
prepared mind.
Louis Pasteur

Arrogance diminishes wisdom.
Arabian Proverb

When the cat mourns for the
mouse do not take her seriously.
Japanese Proverb

Nothing else in the world, not all
the armies, is so powerful as an
idea whose time has come.
Victor Hugo

Knowledge without sense is
twofold folly.
Spanish Proverb

One written word is worth a
thousand pieces of gold.
Japanese Proverb

Wisdom thoroughly learned will
never be forgotten.
Pythagoras

If a word spoken in its time is
worth one piece of money, silence
in its time is worth two.
Hebrew Proverb

The future belongs to him who
knows how to wait.
Russian Proverb

Thinking is the essence of wisdom.
Persian Proverb

Hide not your talents, for use
they were made; what's a sun-dial
in the shade?

Benjamin Franklin

An idea isn't responsible for the
people who believe in it.

Anonymous

Education is what remains when
we have forgotten all that we
have been taught.

Marquis of Halifax

Nothing in life is to be feared.
It is only to be understood.

Marie Curie

A single conversation across the
table with a wise man is worth a
month's study of books.

Chinese Proverb

Words are like leaves;
and where they most abound,
Much fruit of sense
beneath is rarely found.

Alexander Pope

Study without reflection is a
waste of time; reflection without
study is dangerous.
Confucius

The devil can cite Scripture
for his purpose.
William Shakespeare

Natural abilities are like natural
plants, they need pruning
by study.
Francis Bacon

The worst sin toward our fellow
creatures is not to hate them, but
to be indifferent to them; that's
the essence of inhumanity.
G.B. Shaw

Young men think old men are
fools; but old men know young
men are fools.
George Chapman

A vacant mind is open to all
suggestions as a hollow building
echoes all sounds.

Chinese Proverb

It is easier to produce ten
volumes of philosophical
writing than to put one
principle into practice.

Leo Tolstoy

Having a good wife and rich
cabbage soup, seek not
other things.

Russian Proverb

Idealism increases in direct
proportion to one's distance
from the problem.
John Galsworthy

The moment of recognizing your
own lack of talent is a flash
of genius.
Anonymous

Brevity is the soul of wit.
William Shakespeare

Whoever teaches his son teaches
not alone his son but also his
son's son, and so on to the end
of generations.
Hebrew Proverb

Better to remain silent and be
thought a fool than to speak
and remove all doubt.
Abraham Lincoln

Wit without discretion is a sword
in the hand of a fool.
Spanish Proverb

The object of teaching a child is
to enable him to get along
without a teacher.
Elbert Hubbard

When the ship has sunk everyone
knows how she might have
been saved.
Italian Proverb

Whoever would be cured of
ignorance must first confess it.
Michel Eyquem de Montaigne

Women are wiser than men
because they know less and
understand more.
James Stephens

To cultivate a garden is to walk
with God.
Christian Boveé

Fools need advice most, but wise
men only are the better for it.
Benjamin Franklin

An idle brain is the
devil's workshop.
English Proverb

Sometimes you have to be silent
to be heard.
Swiss Proverb

A little nonsense, now and then,
is relished by the wisest men.
Anonymous

It is much easier to be critical
than to be correct.
Benjamin Disraeli

First catch your hare, then cook it.
Anonymous

We cannot all be masters.
William Shakespeare

Proverbs contradict each other.
That is the wisdom of mankind.
Anonymous

Few of the many wise
apothegms which have been
uttered have prevented a single
foolish action.
Thomas Macaulay

Set in Shakespeare roman, designed by
Gudrun Zapf von Hesse exclusively for Hallmark Editions.
Printed on Hallmark Eggshell Book paper.
Designed by William M. Gilmore and Claudia Becker.